HINDSIGHT

ALSO BY ROSANNA WARREN

POETRY

So Forth

De notre vivant, selected poems in French, translated by Aude Pivin

Earthworks: Selected Poems

Ghost in a Red Hat

Departure

Stained Glass

Each Leaf Shines Separate

Snow Day

BIOGRAPHY

Max Jacob: A Life in Art and Letters

CRITICISM

Fables of the Self

TRANSLATION

Euripides, *Suppliant Women*, with Stephen Scully

AS EDITOR

The Art of Translation: Voices from the Field

Eugenio Montale, *Poetic Diaries 1971 and 1972*,
translated by William Arrowsmith

Eugenio Montale, *Poetic Diaries 1974–1977*,
translated by William Arrowsmith

Eugenio Montale, *The Collected Poems of Eugenio Montale: 1926–1977*,
translated by William Arrowsmith

Eugenio Montale, *Cuttlefish Bones*,
translated by William Arrowsmith

Eugenio Montale, *Satura*,
translated by William Arrowsmith

HINDSIGHT

Poems

Rosanna Warren

W. W. NORTON & COMPANY
Independent Publishers Since 1923

Copyright © 2025 by Rosanna Warren

All rights reserved
Printed in the United States of America
First Edition

For information about permission to reproduce selections from this book, write to
Permissions, W. W. Norton & Company, Inc., 500 Fifth Avenue, New York, NY 10110

For information about special discounts for bulk purchases, please contact
W. W. Norton Special Sales at specialsales@wwnorton.com or 800-233-4830

Manufacturing by Versa Press
Production manager: Gwen Cullen

ISBN 978-1-324-11695-0

W. W. Norton & Company, Inc., 500 Fifth Avenue, New York, NY 10110
www.wwnorton.com

W. W. Norton & Company Ltd., 15 Carlisle Street, London W1D 3BS

1 2 3 4 5 6 7 8 9 0

For Adelaide and Lachlan

CONTENTS

I.

A New Year	3
On the Road	4
"Dead Flowers"	5
Number Theory	7
Naturally	8
Burning the Bed	9
Offices	10
Soseki's Shrine	12
Inscription	13
Gall	15
Small Dead Snake	17

II.

"They set about wasting the land"	21
Boletus	22
Kali Yuga	23
Papier-Mâché	25

All Souls' Day	27
Sunfish Midrash	28
In a Strange Land	29
A Heart Sutra	31
The Flood	33
Theseus	35
Iphigenia	36
Such Times	37
Liliane's Scarf	38
Poussin, 1650	39

III.

"Concerning ceremonies,	43
Hindsight	47
Mexico	49
And, till action	50
The Mud Hole	51
The Good Life	52
The Dance	53
Kannon	55
Still Life	57
Illegible	59
Caring	61
Snow	62

IV.

"Summertime"	65
For a New Year	66
In the City:	
Introduction to *The Nature Library*	68
Script	69
Sway	70
Cirrus	71
Equinox	72

NOTES 75
ACKNOWLEDGMENTS 77

I.

A NEW YEAR

Was it myself I left behind? Or was
the country letting go of itself at each clackety-clack
as the train rattled northward into dusk?
Girders flashed by, the ghosts of factories.
Then frozen fields, their stubble narrowly laid out
in an ancient, foreign, indecipherable script.
New solitudes flared on the smutty pane.
As if I were aging faster than the engine's hurtle . . .
While the Hudson shoved its massive, wrinkled drowse
south, dreaming at its own pace: the drowned
river, carrying thousands of years
of sediment through torn uterus of rock.
Angry signs slashed the shadows. Wrecked cars
stacked in yards, tilting fences, sheds
pledged revenge. Then a whoosh of snow
tattered the trees and night swallowed us whole.

Till dawn, jerking me from my berth,
broke over Indiana's frost-bitten furrows,
a country graveyard slotted among farms.

ON THE ROAD

What would you do if, like Don Quixote,
you met Death, an Emperor, a Demon, and a Queen
traveling in a cart along a country road?
It's not every day you encounter the elementals.
Never mind that their faces are pasty with makeup,
their costumes frayed, that they're a troupe of actors
on their way to the next show at a county fair.
Like the Knight of the Sorrowful Face, would you see
through the disguises, into the heart of things?
Beauty makes the heart skip. Power
compels obeisance. But Death is the real
impresario. Remember holding his hand
all night, feeling it stiffen and grow cold in your warm palm.
Until dawn filtered into the room.
And you found yourself alone. When Don Quixote
challenged the actors, they leapt from the cart,
lined up, and prepared to stone him.

"DEAD FLOWERS"

If you hurt yourself before
someone else hurts you, is that
homeopathic? Watch me prick

>   poison into my skin, sign
>   my name in pain. Watch me miss
>   the appointment, cancel the call. Watch me

gulp smoke and receive a certificate
of enlightenment between
the smeared egg-yolk horizon to the west

>   and the bone-white eastern sky:
>   the emperor appoints
>   me to the Poetry Bureau and I

declare myself Queen of the Underground.
On the back road, the turkey vulture
plucked the guts from the squashed squirrel,

>   then flapped up to the dead
>   branch of the shagbark hickory
>   to examine us examining

the carcass. O sacerdotal bird
with your crimson scalp and glossy vestments, teach
us to translate the spasm, the cry, the dis-

>   integrating flesh, the regret.
>   What can be made of all this
>   grief. Over the butter-

yellow, humming, feather-grassed midday meadow
skim the shadows of vultures: ghostly, six-foot
wingspan, V, swiftest signature, turning death into speed.

NUMBER THEORY

The four-and-a-half-foot black-backed rat snake swayed
up and across the kitchen screen door, seeking
a way in. Encountering, instead,

our eyes, it slowly, deliberately, withdrew
to slide across the stone porch, over the wall, and along
the foundation, inspecting every crevice,

feeling, nosing, listening its way
toward a solution, which it found
around the corner, up the back flagstone steps

where it squeezed its impossible length and girth, inch by
patterned inch, into the crack beneath the topmost slate. So
we know we're living with a patient

companion, like you, inquisitive. You sit
taut in your chair, whispering, as you probe
the gaps between prime numbers. Until infinity.

It's pattern you seek. The opening through which
your thought will glide suddenly into a lit space
and be at home. In a shaky house, where wasps gnaw the walls.

NATURALLY

> "I feel that Nature is played out as a Beauty, but not as a Mystery."
> THOMAS HARDY

Rising in the dark for senior pandemic shopping,
we drive east into the spruce-silhouetted dawn
watching the sky stain slowly raspberry as the molten
copper disk of sun floats up over the highway,
a star, a continuous stream of thermonuclear explosions,
one of billions in our galaxy, which is one
among billions of other galaxies, our sun
lighting our way down the exit ramp into the Walmart
parking lot at 6:30 a.m. on planet earth.
We fiddle our masks on over our mammalian noses,
we glove our hairless simian fingers and palms.
Avoiding our masked and fumbling hominid cousins,
we forage along half-empty shelves for relics
of what our sun has fired into vegetal cells. And find
three elderly cabbages, lacking their outer leaves. Browned
in patches, but solid. Their minerals folded into dense
globed dictionaries we will consult and absorb
studiously, in our retreat, for the next three weeks.

BURNING THE BED

Carefully you balanced the old mattress
against the box spring to create a teepee on that frozen December patch
behind the house, carefully

you stacked cardboard in the hollow and touched the match
to corners till flame crawled along the edges
in a rosy smudge before shooting

twenty-five feet into darkening air. Fire gilded each
looming, shadowed tree, gilded our faces as we stood with
   shovel and broom
to smack down sparks. So much

love going up in smoke. It stung
our eyes, our lungs. Pagodas, terraces, domes, boudoirs
flared, shivered, and crumpled

as the light caved in, privacies curled to ash-wisp, towers
toppled, where once we'd warmed each limb,
fired each nerve, ignited

each surprise. And now at dusk, our faces reddened in heat
so artfully lit, we needed all that past, I thought,
to face the night.

OFFICES

In our monastery, crickets rattle
castanets down the long avenues of day and under
the arches of night, in our
monastery squads of dragonflies
patrol the meadow, unzipping
lines of sight while
ferns crinkle into bronze and monardas quail,
Queen Anne's lace frays the surplice of tall grass,
and before Nones the hawk dives into the mountain laurel
   but swerves
up with angry, empty talons, a flash
of white belly feathers and ankle tufts. In our
monastery, before the storm, maples and white pines thrash
with dry heaves, and thunder rackets around
the cloistered horizon as if an enraged dog
had seized the sky in his teeth and were shaking it back and forth
until the stuffing falls out. But in the long
drought days, silences steepen
into abandoned quarries and old wells. The gaps
between your prime numbers pulse like the space between stars.
We live close to the bone.
Your fingers on my spine: primal
shudder of an ancient code. When I rise in the night
and feel my way back to bed in the dark, one hand
on the door, one fumbling along the wall,
it's my mother's ghost who touches me. Do I understand,
now, how she felt in her cavern

of ruined sight? Keep watch, dear Lord, with those who work,
or watch, or weep this night. Hide us
under the shadow of your wings. How slowly
we learn. Compline. In the watches
of the night.

SOSEKI'S SHRINE

The mother bear stands on her hind legs to bat
hard green apples from the boughs, while two cubs
slide up the trunk as if black water should flow
upward and disappear in shuddering leaves.
The third cub rummages for fruit in tall grass.
The apples are tiny and sour. The bears
are hungry, working hard. The whole meadow
strives, shakes with striving, as crickets thrum
and dragonflies slice the air and overhead
the peregrine falcon floats its high, staccato cry.
My fingers are stained with ink. In Kyoto,
in Soseki's ancient temple, the stone basin for mixing ink
stands upright, a shrine to writing. At its base
water in a trough. A dipper. One dips, one pours
water over one's hands. One prays to write
purely. How hard, when we want so much.
We're hungry, we want to leave our names.
"Scholar's hands," the exiled researcher told me,
holding my hands in hers. "Calluses.
Ink stains. Rough cuticles. Hands that work."
She's dead now. Musō Soseki's pond
has lasted for seven hundred years.

INSCRIPTION

and the roots of the fallen oak tree rear
in flamboyant Gothic lozenges: earth sogged
from days of rain so ghost pipes spring up,
crooking their croziers, spectral parasites.
I borrow from them all, sometimes I think
I'm a plant, pale and mycohetero-
trophic. "This is a novel
about time," the learned author declared.
Yes, the Book of Life whose pages
turn slowly yet so swiftly in this
diseased, reclusive year, damp sheets
of shale underfoot and the shuddering silver flash
of beech leaves above. Hardly has the snow
melted than the catalpa's white torches
extinguish and summer starts sliding
into its oubliette. As the black bear
glides so suddenly into the meadow, we never hear
his approach: in a blink
he's here, all presence, a silhouette
tall on his hind legs, smacking apples
from the lower boughs. When he turns,
he shows his Roman snout, his prophetic
brow, his thoughtful, considering eyes.
Like a shadow he springs up the trunk, almost
invisible in the shivering green: he's there,
chomping wild apples, it's his season,
it's their season: let me give away

what I fear, other solstices will roll around:
in childhood I slept in a high room fringed
by dark-sleeved spruces, a tree house in which
I learned a grammar of shadows. That house
is gone, the towering spruces are cut: I hear
the bear munching, the branches shake, it's hard
to distinguish his blackness from the tree's own
inward night. And that larger night I shall be,
oh yes, getting to know.

GALL

Catbirds clawing at the ruby drupes
of viburnum, and bouncing the boughs
as the great heat squats over us and crickets
sandpaper sunlight in the bristling meadow.
We are not lost. We're just quiet.
If we don't speak, it's not that we have
nothing to say. But that the owl
has said it for us in his raspy whistle,
perched twenty feet away on a log fallen
over the brook, professorial, examining
the trickle amid stones. Then suddenly
he drops and seizes—what? a salamander?
in his beak. And gulps it down. A smacking,
cracking sound, after which he fastidiously
wipes his mouth on the trunk. Still more ingenious,
the wasp who drills the oak leaf to lay her eggs,
injecting poisons that swell
the leaf into a gall, a globed papyrus
palazzo in which the commandeered tree
generates a cafeteria so the larvae can feed
until with sprouted wings and feet, lo, they chew
their way out and take flight. They leave
this tea-colored paper lantern ball
Pliny the Elder instructed us to crush and boil with iron
sulfate to make the oak gall ink Europeans wrote with
for almost two thousand years. We are not lost.
We have been writing. Out of our

silence, our bile. Our chafing. Galled.
The larvae were hungry. So was the owl. And we,
from disease, made a codex of hungers
and shaped the letters precisely, so they would last.

SMALL DEAD SNAKE

As when I approached

what I feared and didn't
want to see—the small rat snake curled
where it died struggling in the glue trap set
for mice—
                    and I cried out and twisted my hands but returned
to take up the trap
with gloved fingers, tipped it into a
plastic bag and carried it to the woods on a shovel
                    and dug a hole in dense, root-woven earth,
buried it, then looked up
where tall leafy branches of beech and oak carded
strands of cloud,

so: I tried

to ease with both hands
gently, out of my chest, my fears for you, my
stories about what
                      I feared for you, and tried
to lift the stories free, to place them
out of sight,
beyond the grasp of my belief, beyond horror, but not

beyond

knowing
what traps I had set
for you, for me.

II.

"THEY SET ABOUT WASTING THE LAND"

When the plague first broke out   among
        the Athenians   When the plague

Out of Ethiopia   spread into Egypt   and
        Libya and   among the Persians   Violent

fever   bloody throats and tongues   Vomit
        blisters   foul breath   Genitals

fingers   toes broke off   When the plague   We saw
        the moon rise   It floated

over heaped unburied corpses   Birds
        and dogs that ate them   died   The moon

rose over broken laws   of god and man
        smashed oracles   frantic mortal

orgies   We saw   We heard   words
        turned inside out   Families

broke   Parties passionate for
        power   Crashed   No words were binding   No

oaths reconciled   When the plague
        broke us   We broke   each other

BOLETUS

Crickets are stitching the afternoon
together. What the squalling catbird rends,
crickets relentlessly repair. The maple shivers,
sends yellowed messages sailing down.
Too much has ripped: half the main branch cracked off
and hangs, teetering, across lower boughs
leaving, on the trunk, a blond wound.
We cross the brook on stepping stones and climb
west up the mountain flank through laurel thickets,
along the scooped-out valley of beeches, up
the streambed to sit on a fallen tree. But there's
no rest. We carry with us what we left
below—a country clawing its very idea
to shreds. The scarlet boletus mushroom
prongs from decaying wood. In its bishop's
amaranth skullcap, it stands its ground. One kind
will nourish; the other sickens. But not,
like the white amanita, bringing on
liver failure, seizures, death.

KALI YUGA

The summer of my smashed
vertebrae. The Summer of Love, the vegan cafes
and hippie boutiques of Woodstock still trying
to smoke the weed of 1968
in 2022 as the virus braids
its way in our cells and Russian missiles
blast Ukrainian hospitals into ash.
I tap-tap with my cane along our rutted
North American road past massive oaks,
maples, catalpas, shagbark hickory still
massively green, defying drought, massively
quiet despite gunshot fireworks echoing
coast to coast. The summer
obituaries pile up like unread mail.
Paper to burn. More smoke. I tighten the Velcro belt
of the hospital brace to keep my spine aligned.
I brace myself. *Kali Yuga*, Hindus say:
in the *Mahabharata*, the worst age, the age
of Kali the demon: cataclysm, sin, darkness,
ignorance. How can we find
words beyond our words. Could
the planet burn. You lean to kiss me
because it hurts me to turn. I remember
my back smacking the floor in galaxies
of pain. The summer of bones
knitting their cells across the break. In Wood-
stock in the village square, the guitarist yowled,
amplified, only to himself, but the tinny sound

rebounded decades down the ersatz street.
Summer of ashes, explosions, fumbled words. Of
kale and tofu. Faraway buildings far away tumbling down.
The demon Kali. Over the bodies,
somewhere, summer of someone's love.

PAPIER-MÂCHÉ

He's ripping up a war. The strips
of the *New York Times* slide between his fingers
into the bowl of flour and glue chowder, then splotch
around the balloon where he massages

tanks, missiles, hollow-eyed helmeted men, and
blasted apartments over the swollen skull
of a future pumpkin mask. But pauses
before tearing the page of young recruits,

superhero gear and invincible stances, just like
his comics. He's five years old.
Glue soup spatters his hair, his pants.
He'll make something whole of all this havoc,

the scariest pumpkin we'll ever see.
No bombs fall here. We're free
to shred whole countries on the kitchen floor.
And while we're at it, why not

family feuds, our own mildewed archive
of injury and revenge: what masks
we'll compose from these tatters, this goop,
and when they've dried and we've cut holes

for eyes and painted the crackled frame,
with what new lines of sight we'll squint
at that compulsive brother, Cain,
who acts it out, again, again.

ALL SOULS' DAY

Nobody's running bases or kicking soccer balls across
the scrofulous, moth-eaten municipal playing field,
but you could compose a whole overture in the key of ruddy brick.
Chain link sets the measure, bar by bar.
Where is everyone? We have made ourselves

an enormous fugue. The conductor has withdrawn,
leaving streets, tenements, warehouses, and water towers
to try to remember the rules. Those old Christmas lights
light nothing: half the bulbs are gone. Pylons march
their crucifixes into the choked horizon

where smoke signals waver from factory stacks.
What is man, that thou art mindful of him? Oh, but we're not
entirely alone: two tiny figures are making a deal
in a far corner of the field, and a third approaches.
From such beginnings . . . The wind has its own designs,

lofts its cadenzas high over the grid. Blank scraps.
Or blank to us, who gutter on the ground, without a score.

SUNFISH MIDRASH

"Shall not the Judge of all the earth do justice?"
    GENESIS 18:25

First the spade slicing fat earth, the satisfying heave
of soil onto grass: I poked with my fingers to pull
naked worms. At seven I learned to torture
as I pronged the fishhook into spasming flesh
and dropped it in the stream. And learned to kill—

"If you desire the world to endure, there can be
no absolute justice"—not when I yanked the sunfish
through bright air, hacked off its head
with the not-quite-sharp-enough knife, slit open the narrow
belly, ripped out its guts—all this I learned—

"If you desire": blood on my fingers, I wiped the blade
on the grass, and how the body sizzled
in the pan, my pride and hunger sizzled as I ate—
"absolute justice, the world cannot endure."
"Flying white," a classic Chinese calligraphic

brushstroke, ghost of a figure, not laden
with ink. I still eat fish. I observe the hibiscus,
its pleated white paper satellite dish of bloom
receiving whispered messages from some heavenly
realm where letters aren't shaped in blood.

IN A STRANGE LAND

Not our mountains. Beyond the Chevy junked in weeds
rise snaggle-toothed peaks dimly visible through smoke.
Did we think the landscape would hold still for us?

Sagebrush, lupine, yellow balsamroot, and those small
purple trumpets of sticky geraniums. Five-petaled arnica
heals bleeding wounds. This is grizzly country:

"Use common sense," advises the guide. And what about
those thunderheads rearing up in a celestial Taj Mahal?
Aspens quiver with DTs, alders swish in a *corps de ballet*,

but one whole mountainside is dying a brown death,
a bark beetle–fest. We came a long way
to keep our balance on this rocky ledge,

to stump along the trail trying not to look
a bighorn sheep in the eye. For ages
we've been learning to hold hands, but now I hold

three and a half billion years in my palm, a chunk
of fossil cyanobacteria, the cell
that first churned out oxygen and made our air. You disappear

behind a crag. Each serviceberry leaf a scarlet flame,
a fresh-struck match. Ashes waft
across from Idaho. The Pacific stuck out its foot

and kicked these mountains buckling up into the clouds
where now the cirque in its incisors clamps
the grimy, ragged tablecloth that used to be

a glacier. Tourists since the womb, we cling
to our estrangement, gaping, as the mountain maw
gags and spits one more scrap of ice

thundering into the lake, a bowl of emerald bile.

A HEART SUTRA

If we dragged our suitcases though Shibuya Station, bewildered
by its hundred exits and competing rail lines, and then
shoved our way—following dharma?—through crowds to hesitate

at traffic starfishing in ten directions at Shibuya Crossing, it was not
that we were looking for gods. Nor did the forty-story neon strobe-
flashes strike one spark of divinity.

I set off on my harebrained trek
the next day, alone, pursuing the Four Noble Truths
on two successively intricate subways to debouch

into a long, gray, shabby, graceless street.
"Form is emptiness, emptiness is form," but not here,
where I veered down an alley and stumbled

into a grove of temples and shrines. Stone stairs
invited ascent; a huge bronze bell
tolled the hours in Edo; demons kept watch and preserved
that time.

Realm of desire. Kimonos flowed by,
a scarlet pagoda soared, protected
by the gods of Thunder and Wind and a cumulonimbus

of incense. At the side booths, one hundred yen
procure your fortune on a tiny baton: success

in business, love, fertility, or school exams.

How many reincarnated lives would suffice
for all the rice crackers, candies, trinkets, straw sandals, and bean
    paste buns
for sale in these stalls? While off to the side, among pines,

the Buddhas of Mercy and Wisdom hugely brood.
They exclude nothing. Down the street,
one step past the market, through a gate

in a hidden garden, suddenly quiet, a fountain drips
through evergreen shade where, each alone, a man and a woman
bend their heads. I've flown

halfway around the globe to discover the word No:
no eye no ear no nose no tongue no mind and if
no desire then no suffering nor end

to desire, but instead,
back on the street,
I sink my teeth in a sticky, squirting, reddish bean paste bun.

And taste someone's god, if not my own.

THE FLOOD

—when angels fell out of the bookcase along with old
    newspapers, torn road maps from decades past, and a
                                       prize edition
of the *Très Riches Heures du Duc de Berry*: suddenly

the catalogue tumbled. The painting, the show, Peter Blume's
    Recollection of the Flood, the studio where I slept
as a child those nights when moonlight fingered

the looming canvases, the forest of easels, the jug of brushes
                                         like a spray
    of pussy willow boughs—all surged. In Peter's dream
the restorers stand on scaffolding to paint

the frescoed shapes between lines the flood has spared:
    and won't some massive wave of oil
and shit always storm a city's heart? Restore, restore—

there on the ghostly grid the angels dance
    holding hands in a two-dimensional ballet
of bliss, taking on substance with each cautious dab

to whirl with wings spread over the very rich hours
    of what we've lost. For they are sleeping
on the bench at the foot of the scaffold, the refugees—

the exhausted woman clutching her purse, a scrawny girl
        collapsed in her lap, the huddled, bony old man,
bald head in his hand. And everything they've saved

lies at their feet in a quilt bundle, or stuffed in a box
        tied with twine, or in that suitcase, desperately genteel.
Only the boy is awake. The artist stands

apart. Holds in his hands a sketch we cannot see.
        Blond curls, like Peter's. Remembering, perhaps,
Cossacks, the flight from Russia, the ship, the Brooklyn

tenement where he learned to draw.
        A jug of brushes stands on the windowsill.
The angels keep twirling. I hear, beyond the door,

the growl of mountain streams all dragoning down.

THESEUS

A young king, swashbuckling, expensively schooled
in rhetoric and swordplay, with your gold-threaded tunic and plumed
helmet fitted over your patrician nose:
so you tossed bandits off cliffs and captured a bull—what
do you know
about war? Labor is for peasants, labor pains
for women. But you waded among the suppurating dead
on the fields of Thebes and broke the pollution law
by washing corpses with your own royal hands.
"Which bodies are mine?" I thought, as Bill
Arrowsmith paced back and forth holding out his hands—
"With his own hands!" he kept saying. "Defiled!"
With his own hands he offered us glasses of dark red wine.
We perched along his couch, on his armchairs,
taking notes. We had not yet touched our dead.
Our labors were just beginning, mainly
in library stacks and the pages of dictionaries.
"*Sophrosyne*," Bill barked, "The virtue of moderation,"
with his round, sun-browned, wrinkled satyr's face
and black eyes flashing immoderately
just a few years before he toppled, alone
in his kitchen, his heart ceasing its labors and his corpse
becoming the labor of someone else's hands.

IPHIGENIA

Well I had a whole fleet chafing at the shore
Alliances   Procurement geared up   Provisions
piled in the holds   The men impatient   My brother's
honor at stake   Hell, all our
honors   It was an accident, I didn't
intend harm killing that stag, how could I know
Artemis protected it   I'm feeding an army
for god's sake   Sunlight flashed off
the leaves, my arrow flew straight to its throat
And then   And then   Too many thens
Next thing I know the prophet demands a death
Too much happens in the dark   The unthinkable
until you think it and make a plan
Day after day, no wind, the air heavy upon us like
a mildewed quilt and the men
clamoring   They'd come a long way charged up
for war   An army is a machine it runs
on its own   It's as if the plan
made me   It's not
that I wanted my own daughter on the altar
a garland around her hair, holy water sprinkled
over her head   And that story about the mystical
substitute deer? Don't believe it, the blood
was hers

SUCH TIMES

Crack of the spine against the floor—wave
of nausea, then splintering
pain. How many broken
promises. And where was the Buddha
of Compassion? Covered with dust in the little shop
on Mass Ave just beyond the furniture store
where I fantasized a *vita nuova*.
There were laws to be smashed, a country intent
on doing just that. We lived in such times.
Still, in Prokofiev's piano sonata,
the notes kept rising like a vine on a trellis.
And that, too, was true. There was a way
in which it was true. But did
we hear?

LILIANE'S SCARF

So what's that about, gold chains printed on silk scarves?
And whoever thought women want to be draped
in gold chains? But fabulous sums are spent
on those Chanel scarves. Oh, to be a walking gold mine,
or a gold-bridled thoroughbred, or chained to a bank
vault or a patriarchal name.
Dying, shriveled, alone in her high-ceilinged salon,
enthroned on her couch in a tobacco haze
while the Marie Laurencin watercolor faded slowly
behind its glass, Liliane sent me
her Chanel scarf. To what was she chained?
To *angoisse*—which is not quite anguish. To
the dream of a lost *château*. To the yellow star
pinned to her coat as she walked to school, Jewish,
Parisian, and bound to be hunted down
like her aunts and uncles, cousins, and grandmother, torn
from their apartments, shoved into trucks. I don't know how
to knot this silk stylishly around my neck.

POUSSIN, 1650

I like him looking through me. It's not about
describing. And the way he grips
the portfolio so I can't see
the drawings: you have to deserve
the view. The gold-set agate ring on his little
finger demonstrates his power
to withhold. The studio sinks
into a dun-dung, umber stew.
Fuck the Baroque: let the Romans adorn
their Inquisitional domes with angelic derrières
masquerading as clouds: he'll stick
to the sad geometries of earth. So Phocion's widow
crouches over her husband's ashes and the placid town
putters in the background because who should expect
justice. Keep peace, refuse bribes,
defend the city, tell the truth: no wonder
Phocion made enemies. The only horizon
that counts extends its stoical, shadowed line along
the painter's own mouth. It's no
laughing matter, what he sees in us.

III.

"CONCERNING CEREMONIES,

                              why some
be abolished and some retained": that gold-embossed
Book of Common Prayer (1823) still bears
the scar on the back page where I stabbed
it with a pencil, at age seven, to punish
a sacred I didn't know.
                              Desecration
should invite a response, but
I would live in silence
in my little revolution and "mischievous purposes"
(as the editors put it) "during the late unhappy confusions,"
having stabbed, it appears, only myself.
   *

And so we built a temple, my brother and I.
We dug it into the sandstone bluff at the edge
of the beach, that summer in France.
We thought there should be gifts: we brought
whelk shells, blue sea glass, daisies
drying in a jar. We thought
there should be a god: we carved
a deity, six inches tall, from driftwood
and painted him yellow with a cobalt blue loincloth.
We thought
he should have his own book: we wrote
it in India ink, illuminating in watercolor
his rules, our devotions,

which I no longer remember.
                                  We had
no brass candlestick, no shittim wood, no incense; we soon
turned to other games.
My brother found, in the woods, a German helmet
with a bullet hole blistered through the temple.
And I, walking home from the beach one afternoon,
looked up and saw, where the sky had been,
an absolute blank. And that, too,
was an instruction.

    *

To live in a story? What story?

    *

"The sacrifices of God are a broken spirit——" Mine
wasn't broken. But maimed.
College days. I didn't know
why I no longer ate. I read
books, but the words bled out. I sleepwalked
between classes. The austere doctor,
a Freudian, listened
while I heard myself telling lies
I knew were lies as soon as they flew from my lips.
                                  He
said nothing.

                There are many dead ends.

My heart was not contrite.

"We used to call this *melancholia*," my mother said
coldly.
                    But at winter break, having left
school and the silent doctor and silent books,
I skied alone down the sweep of pasture in the neighbor's farm,
snow-crust cackling under my skis, the dim
elderly mountains crouching around the horizon—

and there, splayed on a barbed wire fence
against that waste of snow,
hung an immense
white, crucified owl. Frozen

where he'd cruised into the wire. His wings
arced like a magician's cape
over the arcanum. He glared
yellowly out of his death. I looked
into the pitiless eyes of a being who was
exactly who he was.
    *

                    And I don't even like Rubens. So why
the ambush? Yes, the flashy brushwork, and who knew more
about the mystery of flesh? But
all those buttocks and bellies, rosacea-
riddled and swollen, the sumptuous folds
of silk, damask, and fur: yet
his Entombment stopped me cold.
White and verdigris, this sagging corpse. And dead
center, where the diagonals cross,

the wound in the ribs. The slit.
Pale blood slithered out. Like
an envelope torn open, that small gash.

                    I think
geometry is the secret—the cut at the heart
of the canvas, the heart of the room, the heart
of—
    what we can't say.

And blood trickled, too, out of the tilted nostrils.
   *

Where is the story?
The story is hidden.
And there are many stories.

Was the letter delivered?
Delivered. But illegible.
   *

"Why some be abolished, and some retained." I,
old now, retain
this savage rite:

              once in a blue moon
to stand heretically at an altar

              and receive

on my tongue the sliver of a broken god.

HINDSIGHT

I've seen demons, each one tossed
in its hurricane of scarf—

they were foreign, carved and painted, they protected
a temple. Shall I invite

one home with his bug eyes, his
fangs? But that's not the conversation

we should be having, you and I:
let's go back to our early letters.

See how ink splurts out
of the capital I? See the tremor

blurring Y-O-U? Each inkblot a cocoon
in which a demon larva battens

and dozes, oozing out its time.
They live for decades in manila folders.

This species is indigenous, en-
dogenous. They secrete

venom. But warmed, scrabbled free,
released to air, they

rise, each new-skeined wing striking an emerald shimmer,
a flash of quartz—
                      I could have

seen you better, I
know that now.

MEXICO

No I didn't chuck out my grandmother, I hardly
knew her. But I lost her books,
those guidebooks to Mexico circa 1908
when she the young gringa bride went riding
among cacti—she had style, my grandmama,
une jolie laide with a broad-brimmed hat—while her husband
   the engineer
tinkered in the Anglo mine until
his heart sputtered. What a romance: they'd never heard
of Zapata. She wore long dresses, blouses with lace.
They lisped their tea. Learned a few words in Spanish.
And the books? Hardcover, mold-ridden, with etchings
of men in sombreros, women in shawls,
donkeys galore. I dragged them from house to house
for decades. Wondering if I'd meet her in those pages.
I never did. And now,
into some dumpster or shunted carton they've vanished,
those ardent, ignorant, Protestant newlyweds
with the long bedragglement that followed
their Mexican fling. How much past
can I do without? Easy to cast off
someone else's illusions. Here, outside
my window in New York, the parchment leaves
of the Callery pear clap in the wind, applauding.
Or is it palsy, shaking them?

AND, TILL ACTION

Castanets in the inner ear, a concert of cicadas
chiming to fanatic sea gods as olive trees

curtsey. Those gods care not
a whit about sexual shame. The face

in orgasm: tragic and
comic mask speckled with foam.

Sacrifice required. The girl will be tossed
from the steed at full surge, lie crumpled

on sand where only hoofprints hem the shore.
We rested briefly on the strand, then rose to shake mica from our hair.

Years later, waves still seethe in the inner ear.
The gods leave traces.

We're streaked and scarred, but still we persevere.
And when, years later, that face startles again

we won't
recognize the beauty we had thought.

THE MUD HOLE

The Mud Hole, we called it, the small dark pond
at the foot of the hill. Earth's eye, omphalos,
secret, canopied by maples, fringed
with brambles, but I knew how to pass
where grown-ups would never find me, perched
in the boughs of the scaly-barked ancestor tree.
A leaf-sprite flecked in shadows, I watched
the frog-rock shoot out its tongue to snag a fly,
the water snake slip through pickerelweed and swivel
in cursive across the murk, the turtle blink
and bask. Lost. Long gone. I climbed carefully down
into the future. Learned to speak human. But still
carry within me the iodine bottle's potion
of pond water, amber, foul, far too potent to drink.

THE GOOD LIFE

Reflecting pool, patio, intricate brick walks and a garden wall—
each time I visited a trellis had been moved, an arbor
transplanted, and inside the house
sofas replaced, walls shifted, plush carpets
reborn in different hues, so that we drifted,
my friend and I, in a metamorphic
universe through which her parents
hovered in rare manifestations like ghosts in a séance,
the father almost invisible, the blonde mother
with haggard quattrocento face surging up from time to time,
then melting away, her speech mysteriously
muffled, never interfering
with our hide and seek, our doll tea parties, our hours
drawing imaginary worlds, and all the while
the gold swans indentured as faucet handles in the bathroom
guarded the master swan from whose gilded beak
a stream of water satisfyingly shot
so that it would be years
before the kingdom dissolved
in a delirium tremens my friend had long since fled,
leaving the grownups to their games of hiding
and seeking, hiding and fruitless
seeking amidst the cloud-capp'd towers and baseless
fabrics of ever-renewed upholstery.

THE DANCE

Was it ritual
that sent the ingénue out onto the dance floor
to step stiffly among the grownups, guided

by the pedagogical hands of her father's friend?
She wore a lavender frock, she didn't
know where to put her feet, the grown-ups moved

like carved wooden figures
gliding out on the hour from a German town hall clock.
The ladies in long rustlements of silk and velvet,

the gentlemen starchily black and white—all
doomed to return, tomorrow, to being human.
As she would return

to studying Latin verbs. There,
she could place her feet. She glimpsed how far
to stretch the future tense. And the subjunctive

mood: possibility,
wish, disguised command—the horizon
gaped. Only years later

would the past take shape. Imperfect,
perfect, pluperfect ran through her fingers
like the gaudy satin strips

she pulled from a trash bin on the Lower East Side:
relics of finery
from an itinerant puppet theater, sashes and flags

of tangerine, magenta, chartreuse, a whole
sunset unfurled in her hands on that
dingy street between the Hell's

Angels' stoop and the Ukrainian coffee shop.
But who
longed for whom? Who tasted ashes? Who

drank bile? The puppet show
had skipped town. With careful steps she advanced
down East Ninth Street, carrying a sunset in her arms.

KANNON
    (For Hannah)

One thousand and one bodhisattvas guard
one dark temple in Kyoto but

you were dying halfway around the world. Tubes
spidered out of your abdomen. Each

bodhisattva needs one thousand arms to hold
the world's lamentations, and that temple needs

one thousand and one Kannons protected by demons
with fangs and flying snakes because

suffering wears many disguises. When we were children
we hacked a garden from weeds at the edge of the schoolyard,

planted marigolds and pansies, and defended the sprouts
with a border of stones. Our fingernails

dirty, our knees mudded. Until the bell
clanged us back to the damage called

History. At our cramped desks with scarred wooden tops.
Our demons not yet grown enough to protect us.

You drew, with each drawing you made
a temple. And tended those rites

with charcoaled fingers and pencil smudges until
your last days, still life, while you still lived—a ball

poised on the bottle's lip, the stuffed
white ptarmigan keeping still. You thought

Kannon helped. When you died alone
on your narrow bed, who else could have gathered

each splintered vertebra, each rip in the lungs, in a shawl
but the thousand-armed one who is both male and female,

who holds arrow, spear, ball, mirror, and moon,
mountain and bed, thistle, mistletoe, and marigolds?

For years, Kannon kept watch.
Kannon, keeper of balances.

STILL LIFE

Not silk roses, but two mackerel
purchased that morning at the stall in Campo de' Fiori
silver but tarnishing
fast, slumped across a plate

I'd set up for art. Their eyes blurred.
Art filled the apartment
with odors of turpentine
and decomposing flesh. Their gills

sagged. Oh, but I was determined.
By the second day they'd sunk
into themselves.
I was eighteen and

virginal. My friend
composed hieratic
bouquets whose silk daisies,
peonies, and roses would never

wilt: her canvas an Egyptian
tomb, and she a priestess.
In my rotting fish I smelled
a future, not yet touched, in which

the man who had held me would turn
away as bonfire-light licked the waves

and someone strummed a lute
and far out beyond the dark harbor

lights from fishing boats blinked. And I knew
I'd spend that night alone
on the damp sand. It was like being born.
At dawn the boats returned:

the fishermen sold their catch, wet starlight,
still twitching,
from tubs along the quay.
Night still aquiver in the fishes' eyes.

ILLEGIBLE
    (In memoriam T.I.)

But the notebook can't clamp shut
over your dying in your armchair and
sitting two weeks before the neighbors

called the police because of the smell.
There's a hole in the story, a hole
in our friendship where you went missing

and I opted for another plot and started
a new journal. They had to
tear out the floorboards under your chair.

Is it a comfort to say
you disappeared before you disappeared?
It's a comfort to

blame. To forget and remember
at the same time—is this what they call
"In Memoriam"? Tanagra figure, Tanagra

face: you danced, collected stones, construed
Greek verbs, you read Aeschylus and heard
Electra praying to Hermes, god

of the Underworld, summoning spirits
from deep in the earth. You summoned,
they came, they crouched among your stones

inviting you into that dark passage
whose shadow falls
at every turn of a page.

CARING

That sprouting apple seed lifted
from the soil in a green hoop, then straightened, its two
tiny palms clamped in a mitten
I took to be dirt. Gallant seedling, shouldering
your way into a world so fraught: I studied you:
how did you muster
that carnival panache, that strongman flair
to shove through earth and hoist into light?
But days passed and still your infant hands were trapped
in their mitt, and I,
so violently helpful, so wanting to see
your flourishing in mine, with my fingernail plucked
off the encumbering clot of dirt, which was not
dirt, but your seed caul, part of your
growing. I lopped
you in half. Such shatterings
do I foist in the name of
care. Here is my plastic
flowerpot. Here is my jaundiced stump of stem.

SNOW

"Your heart is photogenic, but it's shy," the nurse
announces, sliding her jellied wand
over my left breast and under, along the ribs

as the bright green line of my life
scoots and blips and scoots in reassuring intervals
on the TV monitor affixed to the wall.

"I'm truly posthumous," my favorite *enfant
terrible* declared, "and no extra charge,"
but I packed up an entire apartment like practicing

for death. From an old passport, my younger self
stares at me: full-cheeked, with anxious eyes,
she wonders at the crepe paper crinkle above my upper lip,

my cheekbones carved by shadow, my wisping hair.
And I stare back: there's nothing I can tell her,
no warning or advice she'd hear. Em-dashes

scar my diaries. The doctor's screen
shivers in the blizzard static of an ancient black-
and-white TV where snow, once started, falls and falls.

IV.

"SUMMERTIME"

Ash-brown tatters lofted on pheromones,
gypsy moths flutter among boughs and across the meadow
like confetti. Beyond hunger. Only sex
drives the males. The females wait
folded within crevices in bark. They've lost their mouths.
Admirable to be so single-minded.
Just days ago, as creepy adolescents
they chewed the branches bare, littered the path
with skeleton leaf-stalks, tore new craters
out of the canopy so the sky fell through:
we, too, could strip a forest, strip
a continent, but not so lacily.
The lanyard on our neighbor's flagpole clanks
in the wind, the fraying stars and stripes
fluster and droop, maintaining global
dominance in each twitch. The lime-green
katydid impersonates a folded leaf
pressed to the maple trunk, chiding, rasping,
preparing to mate and chew. Along the road
wild Sweet William and purple chicory
festoon derelict beer cans and vodka bottles in the ditch.
We have everything we need, but we want more,
and faster. The crushed garter snake
is scrawled on the tarmac in an ampersand.

FOR A NEW YEAR

Off the paved road, down the dirt track
past trunks of felled ash trees, a crazed giant game
of pick-up sticks jumbling the woods, we come

to the reservoir. The path ends
in the lisp and murmur of wavelets tonguing stones.
Summer ends. A year and a half

of forest retreat will end, and we sit
on driftwood at Rosh Hashanah, watching
late light score the depths with a blade

tarnishing fast. A long horizontal slash
wider than mind. Let's call it peace.
The hills beyond are dozing in muffled blue.

There's a blessing for smelling fragrant spices,
and one for seeing lightning or falling stars, and one
for rainbows, and one for seeing the sea, and putting on

new clothes. There should be one
for the end of a road. The reservoir bears
neither good tidings nor ill, it offers

no sacred knowledge. We sit
quietly. Hearing the slap
of water on rocks. What it reserves

it holds in reserve. We'll make our way
in twilight up the trail, stepping over roots,
past battered, upside-down rowboats wedged between trees

till our shadows
merge with the shades of boughs, boulders, and dangling vines
and a quarry from which night has hacked all the stone.

IN THE CITY: INTRODUCTION TO
THE NATURE LIBRARY

"What do they do?" John Burroughs asked
of creatures. "How do they survive?" I am afraid,
I heard myself say. Snow
dropped in clumps from the boughs of the fir
as if letting go. I have wished,
at times, to let go. And snow falls now
in hectic, crowded, small, determined flakes
obscuring the park, the gates, benches, and pathways
as a helicopter clatters overhead, invisible
but deafening in its mission. In boots and parkas,
firmly mittened, we stroll in public space.
Hard to distinguish, at dusk,
things done from those undone.

SCRIPT

We come on them in the woods, these stone walls
dividing oak from oak, beech from beech
in farmland wrested from forest two hundred
years ago. "The elemental, the primordial,
the silence of the ages," wrote John Burroughs,
already aging in his river-god beard, describing
these rocks "still in motion, creeping down the slopes"
as they did in his boyhood on the Catskills farm
where his father sent him with his brothers
to pry up Devonian chunks and shale to build
fifty rods of wall each year. They penned the sheep
whose wool their mother spun to knit their socks
and mittens, they penned the cow whose milk they churned.
They shot chipmunks, squirrels, hawks, and crows. They rammed
spigots into maple trunks, plowed the rock-toothed fields.
Stone still hunches on stone, shoulder to shoulder
nudged by fingers of moss and lichen, upholstered
by leaf mold, shuddered by frost
while the forest muscles back over
lines still legible but lapsing
into a glacial story we haven't
seen the end of.

SWAY

Determined, forceful, sullen rain—it's almost
made up its mind to be snow. Slush
diving out of the sky: it wants to be seen.
To drive an argument
with the soggy earth. But water holds sway
for now, somersaulting
down the mountain in whorl, froth, and spit, curling back
below each rock like a qualification
or an afterthought.
                        Wind too
has its say: the white pines thrash
in a rave. We walked yesterday
under cumulus domes while lower down, white rags
tore through the air. We're ninety percent
water, cousin to rain, dreaming in crystals, but still

we breathe. The psalmist's whisper tickles our lungs. Our life,
wrote Ruskin, "being partly as the falling leaf,
and partly as flying vapor." Put on your boots,
your parka with its well-lined hood. Amphibious creatures,
we'll scud down the rushing road as sky
flings a mantle of freak white
over the half-thawed ground.

CIRRUS

"I don't have time," I told
myself, "to kill myself: I have
to write a paper on Rimbaud." Which even
at the time I thought funny.
Those were the days I could hardly tell
the difference between hospital and classroom
and walking the dog at 1 a.m.
seemed the only way to preserve an illusion
of balance. Which it did.
Well, that was a long time ago.
Such different tempi now:
as Joel prods the slow,
private smolder in the pile of damp brush, releasing
wisps of blue smoke to waver in air,
the mountain stream pelts over stones, wrinkling silver,
    frothing lace,
ripping laughter out of its own current while
silently moss pries the terrace flagstones apart
and cloud shadows race across the meadow, chased
by slashes of sunlight. In the daffodil spears
thrusting up through dead leaves,
each stalk swells with the pulse of a blossom-to-be.

EQUINOX

The dark-bellied cloud malingers, then
        lifts slowly above the crowns
of the white pines, dragging its skeins
        through their plumes. The late afternoon
lightens in scraps of blue, and treetops waver
        unlike the ledger of my
wrongs and my expert accounting
        of others' misdeeds. Which is called plot.
Three deer wander into the meadow with nothing
        on their minds except the slim
green weeds just poking through winter's straw,
        and in the shiftless light I see again
that young man stripped to his pale waist
        last November in the city, who glided out of the shadows
at the corner of the hotel and the parking lot
        on our nightly walk: a wraith: were we
the strangers he sought? He stood
        watching us pass, with his spindly arms, narrow chest, not
shivering in the almost-winter dark.
        "In our being, God is torn," said Simone Weil.
We walked away, not in his world.

NOTES

" 'Dead Flowers' ": the song by The Rolling Stones.

"Offices": The Offices are the canonical prayers recited in many Christian churches (Eastern and Western) at specific times of day, starting with Matins in the morning and concluding with Compline in the evening.

"Soseki's Shrine": Muso Soseki (1275–1351) was a Japanese Zen Buddhist monk, poet, and founder of several important temples. He is best known for his last temple, Tenryu-ji, in Kyoto, with its famous garden and pond.

" 'They set about wasting the land' ": In the first horror of the coronavirus in 2020, I went back to Thucydides, *The Peloponnesian War*, for its account of the outbreak of plague in Athens and the consequent breakdown of social norms and the corruption of language.

"All Souls' Day" is a tribute to the paintings of John Moore.

"Sunfish Midrash": The commentary on Genesis 18:25 comes from the midrash Genesis Rabbah 39:6: "Rabbi Levi commented, 'Shall not the Judge of all the earth do justice?' If you desire the world to endure there can be no absolute justice. If you desire absolute justice, the world cannot endure."

"The Flood" envisions the painting *Recollection of the Flood* (1969) by the Russian-born American painter Peter Blume. Blume's painting meditates on the flood that savaged Florence in 1966. A study for the painting is in the collection of the Metropolitan Museum of Art.

"Poussin, 1650" is inspired by Nicolas Poussin's *Self Portrait* (1650) in the Louvre, and by his *Landscape with the Ashes of Phocion* (1648) in the Walker Art Gallery in Liverpool.

"And, till action" remembers Shakespeare's Sonnet 129, "Th'expense of spirit in a waste of shame . . ."

"Kannon": The bodhisattva of compassion in Japanese Buddhism, often depicted as androgynous.

ACKNOWLEDGMENTS

I am grateful to the editors of the journals in which these poems first appeared.

The Atlantic: "'Summertime'"

Commonweal: "'Concerning ceremonies,"

The Harvard Review: "Offices"

The Kenyon Review: "Soseki's Shrine," "Inscription"

Liberties: "'Dead Flowers,'" "Burning the Bed," "The Flood," "Theseus"

LitMag: "They set about wasting the land," "Still Life"

The New Republic: "On the Road," "The Mud Hole"

The New Yorker: "A New Year," "Number Theory," "Snow," "Cirrus"

Plume: "Sunfish Midrash," "Hindsight," "And, till action"

Poem-a-Day: "Boletus"

Provincetown Arts: "Kali Yuga," "A Heart Sutra"

Salmagundi: "Iphigenia," "Such Times," "Liliane's Scarf," "Illegible," "Caring"

Sepia Journal: "Kannon"

Smartish Pace: "The Good Life," "The Dance," "For a New Year," "In the City: Introduction to *The Nature Library*"

Revel: "Poussin, 1650," "Sway," "Equinox"

Threepenny Review: "Gall," "Small Dead Snake," "Papier-Mâché," "Mexico"

The Yale Review: "In a Strange Land"

"A New Year" was included in *The Best American Poetry 2024* and in *A Century of Poetry in* The New Yorker *1925–2025*, edited by Kevin Young (Knopf, 2025).

"Naturally" came out in Alice Quinn's anthology of poems inspired by Covid-19, *Together in a Sudden Strangeness: America's Poets Respond to the Pandemic* (Knopf, 2020).

"Offices" was reprinted on the website Poetry Daily on August 11, 2024.

"All Souls' Day" is a tribute to the painter John Moore in the book celebrating him, *John Moore: Portals*, edited by Carl Little (Marshall Wilkes, 2024).

My vivid thanks to the friends who read and pondered some of these poems in early forms: Jonathan Aaron, David Baker, Henri Cole, Alfred Corn, Linda Gregerson, Karl Kirchwey, Phillis Levin, and Loyd Schwartz.

Joel Cohen, my beloved companion, is always my first and cherished reader.

And as ever, my gratitude to Jill Bialosky, who watched kindly and keenly over this book, and to her vigilant assistant, Laura Mucha, and to Jodi Beder, the guardian spirit copyreader.

ABOUT THE AUTHOR

Rosanna Warren taught in the Committee on Social Thought at the University of Chicago from 2012 to 2023 (now Emerita), and previously for many years at Boston University. Her book of criticism, *Fables of the Self: Studies in Lyric Poetry*, came out in 2008. Her most recent books of poems are *So Forth* (2020), *Ghost in a Red Hat* (2011), and Departure (2003). Her biography of Max Jacob, *Max Jacob: A Life in Art and Letters*, was published in October 2020. She is the recipient of awards from the Academy of American Poets, the American Academy of Arts & Letters, the Lila Wallace Foundation, the Guggenheim Foundation, and the New England Poetry Club, among others. She was a Chancellor of the Academy of American Poets from 1999 to 2005 and is a member of the American Academy of Arts and Letters, the American Academy of Arts and Sciences, and the American Philosophical Society. Her poems have been included in twelve editions of *Best American Poetry* and three *Pushcart Prize* volumes.